Field Marks

The Poetry of Don McKay

Field Marks
The Poetry of Don McKay

Selected
with an
introduction by
Méira Cook
and an
afterword by
Don McKay

LAURIER POETRY SERIES

Wilfrid Laurier University Press

We acknowledge the support of the Canada Council for the Arts for our publishing pro-gram. We acknowledge the financial support of the Government of Canada through the Book Publishing Industry Development Program for our publishing activities.

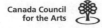

Library and Archives Canada Cataloguing in Publication

McKay, Don, 1942–

   Field marks : the poetry of Don McKay / selected, with an introduction by Méira Cook ; and an afterword by Don McKay.

(Laurier poetry series)
Includes bibliographical references.
ISBN-13: 978-0-88920-494-2
ISBN-10: 0-88920-494-2

   I. Cook, Méira, 1964–   II. Title.   III. Series.

PS8575.K28F518 2006   c811'.54   C2006-901198-2

© 2006 Wilfrid Laurier University Press
Waterloo, Ontario, Canada N2L 3C5
www.wlupress.wlu.ca

Cover image: Brian Henderson. *Quail*, 1999. Colour photo.

Cover and text design by P. J. Woodland.

Every reasonable effort has been made to acquire permission for copyright material used in this text, and to acknowledge all such indebtedness accurately. Any errors and omissions called to the publisher's attention will be corrected in future printings.

∞

This book is printed on 100% post-consumer recycled paper.

Printed in Canada

Table of Contents

Foreword

At the beginning of the twenty-first century, poetry in Canada—writing and publishing it, reading and thinking about it—finds itself in a strangely conflicted place. We have many strong poets continuing to produce exciting new work, and there is still a small audience for poetry; but increasingly, poetry is becoming a vulnerable art, for reasons that don't need to be rehearsed.

But there are things to be done: we need more real engagement with our poets. There needs to be more access to their work in more venues—in classrooms, in the public arena, in the media—and there needs to be more, and more different kinds of publications, that make the wide range of our contemporary poetry more widely available.

The hope that animates this new series from Wilfrid Laurier University Press is that these volumes will help to create and sustain the larger readership that contemporary Canadian poetry so richly deserves. Like our fiction writers, our poets are much celebrated abroad; they should just as properly be better known at home.

Our idea has been to ask a critic (sometimes herself a poet) to select thirty-five poems from across a poet's career; write an engaging, accessible introduction; and have the poet write an afterword. In this way, we think that the usual practice of teaching a poet through eight or twelve poems from an anthology will be much improved upon; and readers in and out of classrooms will have more useful, engaging, and comprehensive introductions to a poet's work. Readers might also come to see more readily, we hope, the connections among, as well as the distances between, the life and the work.

It was the ending of an Al Purdy poem that gave Margaret Laurence the epigraph for *The Diviners*: "but they had their being once / and left a place to stand on." Our poets still do, and they are leaving many places to stand on. We hope that this series will help, variously, to show how and why this is so.

—*Neil Besner*
General Editor

Biographical Note

Born in Owen Sound, Ontario, in 1942, Don McKay was educated at the universities of Western Ontario and Wales, where he earned his Ph.D. in 1971. He taught English and Creative Writing at Western and the University of New Brunswick for twenty-seven years before retiring to write poetry full time. McKay has long enjoyed a celebrated reputation as a mentor to other writers; he has worked at the Sage Hill Writing Experience in Saskatchewan and at the Banff Centre for the Arts. He has also been prominent as an editor and a publisher: with Stan Dragland, he was the founding publisher and editor in 1975 of the small Ontario press Brick Books, one of Canada's leading poetry presses, and he edited the well-known literary journal *The Fiddlehead* at the University of New Brunswick from 1991–96. After his teaching career, McKay settled in Victoria with his partner, the poet and philosopher Jan Zwicky.

McKay's poetry has won many honours and prizes, including two Governor General's awards, for *Night Field* (1991) and *Another Gravity* (2000). He was nominated for the prestigious Griffin Prize in 2004. His first book of poems, *Air Occupies Space*, appeared in 1973; other volumes include *Long Sault* (1975), *Lependu* (1978), *Lightning Ball Bait* (1980), *Birding, or Desire* (1983), *Sanding Down This Rocking Chair on a Windy Night* (1987), *Night Field* (1991), *Apparatus* (1997), *Another Gravity* (2000), and the chapbook, *Varves* (2003). His most recent book is the collection *Camber: Selected Poems 1983–2000* (2004).

Introduction

Song for the Song of the Dogged Birdwatcher

Award-winning poet, essayist, critic, beloved teacher and professor, Don McKay taught English and creative writing at The University of Western Ontario and the University of New Brunswick before moving to Victoria with his partner, acclaimed poet Jan Zwicky. McKay has worked as poetry editor for *The Fiddlehead* magazine, manuscript reader for Brick Books, and poetry facilitator at The Banff Centre; he has twice won the Governor General's Award, for *Night Field* (1991) and *Another Gravity* (2000). Readers, students, browsers, and loiterers between the pages of McKay's poems are fortunate in their access to a fine poet who is lyrical, wise, and winsome in his writings on nature, birdwatching, wilderness poetics, and the homing instinct in, amongst other things, his eccentrically philosophical field guide *Vis-à-Vis: Fieldnotes on Poetry and Wilderness* (2001). Although bonded by nothing so categorical as a "school," McKay's environmental poetics, his peculiarly gentle, un-grasping, disowning brand of nature poetry has often been grouped with that of poets such as Tim Lilburn, Dennis Lee, Roo Borson, Robert Bringhurst, and Jan Zwicky—ecologically centred poets inspired by the conflict between inspiration and gnosis, instinct and knowledge.

On Birding

> Sparrows burning
> bright bright bright against the wind
> —"Adagio for a Fallen Sparrow"
> (*Birding, or Desire*)

McKay is an avid birdwatcher, and his poetry is alive, *bright*, with the pres-ence of birds—imagined, metaphoric, in flight, grounded, winging it across southern Ontario skies or pressed, wildflower-like, between the stern pages of the hobbyist's field guide: *The Birds of Canada*. Indeed, this reference guide becomes something of a quirky leitmotif entangled in the pages of *Birding* as its earnest, binocular-gazing protagonist lopes across fields and streams, peering into thickets and over hillocks. The point, as many critics have remarked (Bondar, Elmslie, Oughton), is that McKay's self-effacing poetic persona is never far from this slightly stumbling, stooped and wandering, peripatetic birdwatcher. Birding—implying the act of watching birds and the act of *being* a bird—hints at a presumptive metamorphosis from which McKay's persona swiftly dissociates himself. For this humble watcher, birding (like reading, like writing poetry) is an act of attentiveness, a working poetic in which the attendee "discovers" but never appropriates the wilderness world. Gingerly, tactfully, reverently, McKay's watcher never "becomes" bird.

Who, then, is the birdwatcher? Or, rather, who is the poetic persona in his guise of birdwatcher preoccupied in translating the free-fall and thrall, the lift of bird into language, that allows us to imagine the feathered imperative of draft and drift, that locates our readerly flight path, our freedom to fly or fall? Oblique, evasive, learned, witty, wry, whimsical, McKay's birder is viewer rather than voyeur, his place in language, in landscape, a subtly achieved, precariously wrestled subject position in which poetic flight constitutes the sum of "knowing where and how to land within language" (Bondar 20). The characteristic sideways lope of such poetry depends upon an eccentric point of view, serviced by a compassionate yet utterly curious poetic presence, lending intimacy to the most detached observations. In his essay on nature poetry, "Baler Twine," McKay addresses this intensification of poetic attention as "a species of longing … without the desire to possess" (*Vis-à-Vis* 26). Knowing absent of appropriation, instinct empty of grasping: these are the human attributes McKay celebrates in his attentiveness to the "wilderness."

Such "wilderness knowledge" is always leavened by humour. The explicit "birdwatcher" poems in McKay's oeuvre ("Field Marks:" and "Field Marks (2):" in *Birding*) provide the funniest, most ironic accounts of the droll bird-watcher beset with complicated accoutrements traipsing through a landscape more textual than natural:

> Wears extra eyes around his neck, his mind
> pokes out his ears the way an Irish Setter's nose
> pokes out a station-wagon window.
> His heart is suet. He would be a bird book full of
> lavish illustrations with a text of metaphor. (15)

The "egghead" who "wings it" in the opening poem has so far progressed in learning that by "Field Marks (2):" he is able to assign birds to their proper categories without in the least appreciating "that birds have sinuses through-out their bodies, / and that their bones are flutes" or that "every feather is a pen, but living, / flying" (75).

This birdwatcher is deaf to the living resonances between birds and feathers and flutes and pens, insects and their frequencies, swallows and their soarings. At the same time, McKay's inept birdwatcher, who compares the "shape and texture" of "her thigh" to a "snowy egret's neck," who "utters absolutes he instantly forgets," may be compared to the poet-persona conjuring romantic metaphors from "her thigh," an "egret's neck," a "swallow's evening." Certainly, it is tempting to observe in this opening poem in *Birding* the gently mocking conjunction of birdwatcher with poet-persona, an association that emphasizes the off-handed, likeably self-mocking, endearingly modest poetic presence behind these poems.

As for birding, so for wording.

Like reading and writing, birding transforms into mental migration, an elaborate metaphor for the poetic process. The bird itself, that hollow-boned creature, "dense with otherness" (Dragland 883), lends itself to an openformed lyricism in which poems gather flight paths, locate tensile rhythms, stretch time and compact space; turning from flight into metaphor:

> There are
> birds no one has ever seen
> uncaged in any book unguessed
> by metaphor.
> —"The Night Shift"
> (*Sanding Down This Rocking Chair*)

In *Another Gravity*, gravity is title and technique, the co-efficiency of drag, the slow gagged pull of solemnity (encompassing the force by which bodies are drawn to earth's centre as well as their ability to bear moral weight, gravity, gravitas). And flight? If gravity refers to what is *material* in language then flight is all metaphor, all leap and longing, all air and stare and star. Read one of my favourite poems, "Dreamskaters," for a thoroughgoing experience of poetic flight:

> , chasing chance with all the moves
> of swallows swirling to
> connect, their physics
> liquified by knives, carving and
> releasing from the ice the cold
> caught music of the river, stroke, stroke,
> just have time to scribble you this note then
> scissor and wheel syncromesh to long
> parabolas of sense they pour and
> drink their speed those

> tossed off phrases those
> sky readers those high
> raptors
>
> (*Birding, or Desire*)

In loping, associative lines, McKay describes his dreamskaters crossing back and forth across ice or sky. While this poem is not about real birds—and while we may be uncertain if the skaters are themselves real, imaginary, or surreal—metaphorical swallows swirl past while language raptors toss off phrases from on high.

In the same volume McKay includes five numbered poems about (real) swallows entitled "Swallowings," in which swallows are compared to schizophrenic thoughts, snickersnacks of the air, and aeronautical birds. Yet swallows and their idiosyncratic swallowings comprise the primary comparative term in these metaphors: it is the *swallows* that are real. In "Dreamskaters," however, McKay produces a poem of pure flight that is not about flight, in which birds are wholly absent except as metaphor but fully present because of the force of their imaging. Try reading "Dreamskaters" without scimitars of swallows' wings curving between you and the skaters, the rapture of raptors ringing off steel blades. Just try.

"Dreamskaters" encrypts flight as metaphor while in "Alibi" (*Apparatus*) flight is the impossible, inexpressible anti-metaphor it has become imperative to write:

> Because the swallows had departed from the cliff,
> over and over,
> the soft knives of their wings tasting the river mist as they
> went wherever it is
> they went... (19)

The oxymoronic phrase "soft knives" is only one indication of the poet's anxiety, the poet's difficulty in describing flight, what he haltingly specifies as:

> the long dread
> carpentry of history, and then, and so, and so,
> and then, each bone nailed, wired, welded,
> riveted... (19)

The upsurge and banking momentum of these words search out their own thermal currents, what McKay in "Sometimes a Voice" will wonderfully name "troubled air, a flight path still / looking for its bird" (*Another Gravity*).

Similarly, McKay's poetics utilize sound rhythms, alliteration, tone leading, and onomatopoeia to echo the lift and ballast of flight, float, and fall. The following excerpt from "Hush Factor" demonstrates his skilful sounding(s) of the night-shifting wide-winged *silence* of the barred owl's flight:

> Rogue translation. Out of lullaby and slow
> cathedral air to wrench this barely
> thickened sibilance and make it mean
> the sudden death of sound: *hush.*
>
> (*Another Gravity*)

The ironic act of symbolizing silence through acoustic devices awakens McKay's reader to the idea that language continually strives to abridge the misprision between wilderness worlds and their human equivalents.

On Metaphor

> The excitement of metaphor stems from the injection of wilderness into language; it is quick, tricky, and, as we have seen, not easily domesticated to utility.
> —Don McKay
> (*Vis-à-Vis*)

Previously the discussion of flight led to the notion of metaphor as an attempt to break free of language and the literal. Metaphor is the part of speech that allows language to fly just as hollow bones and primaries are the parts of birds that do likewise. Fly.

> Bird, that is.
> Soar and shine within the stern buoyancies of language. Metaphor,
> that is.

Metaphors electrify a poem with sound and sense, and promote startling leaps that wrest the reader from habitual associations. In an early critical essay on Dylan Thomas concerned with Thomas's shape-changing imagery ("Crafty Dylan" 36), McKay refers to "the trickster's tongue in the poet's cheek," and in a recent essay on poetics, "Remembering Apparatus," McKay meditates subtly upon this metaphor trickster, this raven of language: "Thanks to metaphor, we know more; but we also know that *we don't own what we know*" (*Vis-à-Vis* 69, McKay's emphasis). Metaphor with its false, often irrational claims, McKay reminds, somehow produces authenticity, profundity, even truthfulness:

                                                    look
          The Great Blue Heron
          (the birdboned wrist).
                          —"The Great Blue Heron"
                                (*Long Sault*)

What does that "small / manyveined /wrist" earlier in this poem have in
common with the great blue heron besides their proximity on the page and a
certain spurious bird-boniness? Their commonality resides in the metaphoric
juxtaposition that is greater than the sum of their parts and that imparts a
poignant, half-lost, flickering sadness to the scene, a scene illuminated by the
perishing light of memory and anchored solely by the touch of father's hand
on child's wrist—*look*!—upon the gunwale. "The sadness of metaphor,"
writes McKay, "stems from an awareness of lost things as we waken to the
teeming life outside the language we inhabit" (*Vis-à-Vis* 72).

     Critics have long considered McKay a virtuosic metaphoriste (Coles,
Forster, Goulet). Kevin Bushell usefully distinguishes between metaphors of
low tension and those of heightened tension, the latter being the characteristic
configuration favoured by McKay. Because of tension created between objects
of comparison, between focus and frame, "high tension" poetry promotes
startling metaphoric effects, encouraging imagistic torque not readily legible
in more habitual phrasing.

     Metaphors describing cerebral states abound in McKay's oeuvre, inevitably
attracting "high tensile" comparisons. "Whose idea was it / to construct a
mind exclusively of shoulders?" enquires the fretful protagonist of "Song for
the Restless Wind" (*Night Field*) while in "Grief and the Sea," "The sad / shop-
ping cart of the mind imagines / dumping its confections" (*Apparatus*), and in
Lependu the mind is "a flock of blackbirds flapping behind my eyes." Neither
ornamental nor entirely rational, McKay's metaphors breach decorum, logic,
convention, and expectation. Startling, jubilant, joyful, these metaphors stand
in the place of failure—failure in logic, similitude, denotation—instead
forging a fertile negotiation with otherness, the non-human, the extra-lin-
guistic, what McKay has named the space of "wilderness." This riddling trope
of fluidity, this raven-flight between startling and illogical comparisons, this
"trickster's tongue in the poet's cheek" most truly rewards our attentive
listening.

     When McKay writes about authentic moments of engagement shorn of
ego or appropriative desire, as he does in "The Great Blue Heron," the reader
experiences various "shifts in seeing" however vast, however minute. This last
phrase composes the opening line of "Migratory Patterns," a poem that sends
word of a bird we've met before:

a friend writes
of a Great Blue Heron hunting in the moonlight, stalk and bend
and stab along the ordinary beach, sewing a scene
past dreaming

(*Birding, or Desire*)

"One metaphor" writes McKay, "for the excitement of metaphor is to say that they are entry points where wilderness re-invades language, the place where words put their authority at risk" (*Vis-à-Vis* 85). Or, if you prefer: a crisp, eight-line poem beginning with the sidelong glance and, two astonishing metaphors later, ending with the image of a "white flag flashed" imprinted upon the startled retina:

and came that morning down the dusty road
into the deer's
virginity—
        gone, white flag flashed
did you see it flashed
like a
like a fridge left crisp & clean in the mind
all day
        "—deer"
        (*Long Sault*)

The collision of natural and manufactured elements—deer's tail with flag and fridge—is heightened by hesitation, the stammer in the sixth line. The incongruity of comparison, the high-tension metaphors confer the unexpected jokiness of a punchline upon the poem.

McKay's associative leaps from concrete language to abstract ideas, his comparisons of what is "natural" to what is cultural, technological, artificial, constructed, produce new meanings not easily paraphrased. His metaphors bear ontological significance, for they do not merely uncover the world but *discover* it, leading the reader into new (if illogical, if experimental, if wild, if *wilderness*) areas of experience and (un)knowing.

Metaphors cross-section McKay's poetry, but despite their will to knowledge and profundity and clarity, metaphors inevitably resist conferring full meaning upon their subject(s). Says McKay: "metaphor's first act is to unname its subject, reopening the question of reference" (*Vis-à-Vis* 69). In the midst of such instability, such writerly ambiguity, it is inevitable that a residue of inexpressible meaning persists; the metaphor, despite its animation and vibrancy and power to startle, remaining essentially insoluble.

On Nature Poetry

McKay's early poem, *Long Sault*, taking as its setting the construction of the hydroelectric dam at Cornwall, Ontario, during the late fifties (the St. Lawrence River flooded upstream submerging a length of shoreline) represents nature eluding captivity, nature as it roils and rolls, flows, flees, and froths with the water system running through the town. In addition, poems that detail and explicate the natural world, landscape and its creatures, may also be classified as nature poetry, as in the case of the pedagogically precise "Meditation on a Geode":

> Once upon a time there was a little animal who lived and
> died, got buried in the silt and gradually decayed to nothing,
> which filled up with water
>
> *(Night Field)*

and the delicately frangible "Some Functions of a Leaf ":

> to starve in technicolour, then
> having served two hours in a children's leaf pile, slowly
> stir its vitamins into the earth.
>
> To be the artist of mortality.
> *(Sanding Down This Rocking Chair)*

Yet, McKay's notion of "nature," of "wilderness," does not confine itself only to what grows "naturally" in the "wild." The poet "may be focused on the wilderness in a car, a coat hanger, or even language itself" he writes, maintaining that the landscape of the nature poet stretches all the way from "front lawn to back country" (*Vis-à-Vis* 26). Reviewer Jay Ruzesky emphasizes this point: "His territory is the natural world but includes the points where civilization impinges on the hinterland" (126). Such "impingement," the startling collision of wilderness civility and civilized bewilderment, includes lonesome strips of highway as in "Art's Auto Rad" (*Night Field*) and "On Foot to the ByPass Esso Postal Outlet" (*Apparatus*), the garden with its bricolage of yard-sale rummagings, suburban sprinklers pulsing "back and forth salaam salaam" in "August" (*Lependu*), and the typical McKay-ian image of backyards blurring into wilderness scrub as in "Sunday Morning, Raisin River" (*Apparatus*).

In poems such as "Down River, Into the Camp" (*Air Occupies Space*) and the oddly ironic section from "Nostra" beginning "The wrong rough road"

(*Night Field*), a protagonist canoes or hikes or drives into an unexpected clearing in scrub or bush or scruff and discovers a wilderness which, although apparently "civilized" by campers, is revealed as stranger, more chaotic and sinister than the brush he has traversed to get there.

The wilderness McKay's poetry discovers in landscape, creatures, faces, tools, and objects bespeaks a lyrical encounter with otherness, with what is non-human or alien as well as the resulting disproportion, incongruity, and incomprehensibility of these encounters. Such confrontations may be uneasy, disordered, even chaotic, but they are always illuminated by humility and respect, by "a mind / widen [ing] with expectancy" in the words of "Le Style" (*Sanding*). For McKay, the wilderness is clearly not a circumscribed category of endangered species but rather:

> The capacity of all things to elude the mind's appropriations ...
> the sudden angle of perception, the phenomenal surprise which
> constitutes the sharpened moments of *haiku* and imagism. The
> coat hanger asks a question; the arm-chair is suddenly crouched:
> in such defamiliarizations, often arranged by art, we encounter
> the momentary circumvention of the mind's categories to glimpse
> some thing's autonomy—its rawness,—its *duende*, its alien being.
>
> (*Vis-à-Vis* 21)

Thus the quality of "wilderness" may be found in all things, residual in objects, machinery, in lever and hinge and rotor cuff. When reading McKay's wonderful "tool" poems such as "Choosing the Bow," "Meditation on Shovels," and "Canadian Tyre" (*Night Field*) or, later, "Early Instruments," and "Setting the Table" (*Apparatus*), one is aware of the humming, grunting, panting "animal inside the instrument" which might "muffl(e) the perfections of hammer, pedal, / wire, the whole / tool kit" but which animates the instrument beyond, far beyond, the mind's appropriations ("Glenn Gould, Humming," *Apparatus*). For this is a poet, remember, who longs to be fondly remembered, *loved*, by every object he has ever handled.

Objects—thing-ity, made-ness—preoccupy McKay with their secret wilderness life, a life, he remarks, that accumulates "a kind of static electricity through a life-time of rubbing against people" ("Impulse to Epic" 32). Observe, for example, the apparently domesticated farmyard scene in "The Night Shift," rendered unfamiliar, "object-ified" by darkness (*Sanding*). In a world of object and creature made strange where flowers "begin inhaling through their roots / exhaling darkness," the static electricity of the everyday is transformed into a malign current, undomesticated by the mind's categories.

Notes McKay in his foreword to the Wilderness issue of a national journal:
"Perhaps wilderness is not so much a dwindling set of shrinking places as the
capacity in all things, even tools, to elude us, to outfox the mind's appropri-
ations" (5).

And language? In McKay's poetry of homage toward our intimate relation-
ship with objects where does language fall, falter, hold fast, or fail? Predictably,
language composes itself as tool and as wilderness-yearning: "To think of
language as apparatus, to use and inhabit it with an awareness of residual
wilderness" (*Vis-à-Vis* 62).

In McKay's wilderness thinking, on the threshold between intuition and
knowing, "nature" is not confined to parklands, neither is the "wild" a demar-
cated off-track area. Instead, nature unfolds within us, and wilderness poetics
partakes of bird, leaf and tree, tool, tractor, truck, language, leaving, and lost-
ness. Witness McKay, finally, "On Leaving:"

> On leaving, you circulate among the things you own
> to say farewell, properly,
> knowing they will not cease to exist
> after your departure, but go,
> slowly, each in its own way,
> wild.

> (*Another Gravity*)

On the Open Hand

> To make a home is to establish identity with a primordial grasp, yes;
> but it is also in some measure, to give it away with an extended palm.
> —Don McKay
> (*Vis-à-Vis*)

Homing withholds connotations of cozy domesticity in McKay's writing,
emphasizing instead the extension of self into world together with a resistance
to acts of ownership, colonization, even of naming: "When ownership is set
aside, appropriation can turn inside out, an opening, a way of going up to
something with a gift from home" (*Vis-à-Vis* 31). McKay's "excursionist
poetics" (Elmslie), his poems of ambling, wandering, and meandering, of
taking the wrong road and getting "there" anyway—"Got to meander if you
want to get to town," muses the browsing *bricoleur* of "Canadian Tyre"—of
deviation, digression, excursion in landscape, and incursion in language,
represent various ways of knowing without claiming, colonizing, domesti-
cating, or grasping.

A *flâneur* of the wilderness, of space and system and syntax, an excursionist in language—read "New Moon" (*Another Gravity*) as etymological flight—a linguistic adventurer receptive to contingency, exploration, and wilderness-thought, McKay creates a poetics that foreswears ownership, claims of possession, possessiveness, and the hand's primordial grasp. Instead, his is the poetry of attentiveness, courtesy, homage. One imagines his quality of watchfulness as a radical unselving, a self-deprecating duck-and-parry, a partial effacement the better to approach otherness:

> Inertia inside motion
>
> as the stone
> inside the cherry: I stand
>
> handful of seed outstretched
> waiting for the black-capped
>
> nothing-at-all to flirt up
> perch on my finger
> —"Plantation"
> (*Night Field*)

This refusal to name the species for which the speaker waits as anything more specific than "black-capped / nothing-at-all" is a playful gesture, a bit of "anthropomorphic play" in McKay's words (*Vis-à-Vis* 31), as well as a serious commentary on failed naming(s): "But even 'apt' names touch but a tiny portion of a creature, place, or thing ... the abject thinness of language" (*Vis-à-Vis* 64).

Frequently, McKay's poetry bespeaks a longing to eschew this "abject thinness" of nomenclature, this dour naming of parts:

> It would be nice to write the field guide for those riverbanks,
> to speak without names of the fugitive
> nocturnal creatures that live and die in our lives.
> —"Another Theory of Dusk"
> (*Night Field*)

McKay is not attempting to divide nature from culture, writing from riverbanks, field guides from fields. Instead, what he has named "this crisis in the naming of things" has proven an obstacle to poetic speech, to the open hand, to courtesy and response and responsivity, to "the business of naming with this listening folded inside" (*Vis-à-Vis* 64, 66). Fellow poet-philosopher, Tim Lilburn, states the case pre-emptively:

The world is its names plus their cancellations, what we call it and
the undermining of our identifications by an ungraspable residue
in objects. To see it otherwise, to imagine it caught in our phrases,
is to know it without courtesy, and this perhaps is not to know it
at all. (163)

McKay's gentle poetics of reverence towards the hidden wilderness in
creature and thing partakes of such courtesy yet his poetry is precise, allusive,
particular, accurate. As Robert Bringhurst remarks, McKay breaks with the
tradition of rapturous, non-specific, pantheistic nature poetry inaugurated—
perfected—by Wordsworth. Where Wordsworth might recollect in tranquility
images of "tree" or "bird," McKay painstakingly describes "white pine, red
pine, loon, or Blackburnian warbler" (Bringhurst 31).

Indeed, as nature poet his genealogy more accurately derives from that
ecstatic, austere poet-priest, Gerard Manley Hopkins. McKay's poem
"Buckling," for example, pays explicit tribute to Hopkins's "The Windhover,"
McKay's windhover reviving phoenix-like by dint of the "quick lift of caffeine"
before "sliding a talon through the sweet flesh of your fist" (*Sanding*). Add
to this numerous poems preoccupied with (un)naming, genealogy, kinship,
category, and the reticulated "casting outward" of that "muscle we long with?
Spirit?" ("Twinflower," *Apparatus*). Ironically, "Twinflower" provides a
fascinating gloss on the naming of species, both as categorical enterprise
and as ontological imperative:

> Listen now,
> *Linnaea borealis*, while I read of how
> you have been loved—
> with keys and adjectives and numbers, all the teeth
> the mind can muster. How your namer,
> Carolus Linnaeus, gave you his
> to live by in the system he devised.
>
> . . .
>
> Then God said, O.K. let's get this show
> on the road, boy, get some names
> stuck on these critters, and Adam,
> his head on the ground in a patch of tiny
> pink-white flowers, said
> mmn, just a sec.

When the wilderness within language chimes with the respect accorded
to nature then, *then* the sullen naming of parts McKay has gently ridiculed

gloriously falls away. Finally, these poignant lines from "Load," a poem that witnesses the speaker's witnessing of a white-throated sparrow huddled in flight-exhaustion:

> I wanted
> very much to stroke it, and recalling
> several terrors of my brief
> and trivial existence, didn't.
> (Another Gravity)

Like laughter, like grief, like birds, nature, landscape, and language, the poet knows such things cannot be domesticated and because they cannot be, he doesn't.

On Language

> All poetry calls its readers into being.
> —Don McKay
> ("What Shall We Do?")

What is the place of language in nature, in nature poetry? Language—as artifice, frame, metaphor, music, humour, and so on—translates the not entirely silent but possibly less than intelligible world of nature from poet to reader. Witness "Some Exercises on the Cry of the Loon:"

> Write a book about it
> and tear out all the pages.
> Drop your rake and jump into the ditch, then
> climb out and continue raking. Show them
> intermittence is more elegant than suicide.
> (Birding, or Desire)

In lines shapely and sufficient, as if turned on a carpenter's lathe, McKay erases our familiarity with birdsong, with the habitual cry of the loon. This disjunction ensures that the reader's perception does not travel transparently into language. Instead, a palpable break occurs, an incongruity between the subject of the title—loon's plaintive cry—and the variety of creative yet aberrant ways by which this cry is sounded and resounded in language, in the "extra metaphorical stretch and silliness of language as it moves toward the other" (*Vis-à-Vis* 31).

Rather than recreating bird song onomatopoetically, as he has elsewhere done, McKay's self-reflexive lines envision a symbolic life for the loon's cry, simultaneously critiquing poetry's ability to transcribe "life" into language, song into symbol, flight into form, and artlessness into an aesthetics of image and desire. In this context read "How to Imagine an Albatross" (*Sanding*), which explicitly aligns the construct of "bird" with the flickering (un)reality of "image," or "Meditation on Snow Clouds Approaching the University from the North-West," in which clouds represent birds flying high as ideas, becoming the poem's *cogito* that will prove the *ergo sum*:

> The clouds look inward, thinking of a way
> to put this. Possibly
> dying will be such a pause:
> the cadence where we meet a bird or animal
> to lead us, somehow,
> out of language and intelligence.
>
> (*Night Field*)

These poems of thrilling misalignment between image and idea—an entire subset exists in McKay's oeuvre—these meditations on the persistence of otherness and the sincere, *wrenching*, always elusive quality of language to slake this otherness (of creature, object, landscape) represent one of McKay's deepest poetic convictions. In the long poem "Nostra," he expresses such fleetingness as "Thoughts / that pass through language as the sun through water" (*Night Field*). Images of the transparent diversity of different mediums—sun through water, thought through language—illuminate our creaturely difficulty with what is alien, other: "the disturbing, thrilling awareness that there really is a world outside language which, creatures of language ourselves, we translate with difficulty" ("Local Wilderness" 6).

How perception may be altered by what is visual/visionary remains a source of wonder in McKay's poetry, and a record of his poetics would be sorely one-sided without an account of the broad range of sensory responses by which he derives the improvisatory, humorous qualities that distinguish his writing. In this context, enter *Lependu*, a sequence of twenty-three linked yet self-sufficient poems exuberantly relating the story of Cornelius A. Burley's execution by hanging in Ontario in 1830. Having broken the rope, Burley is hanged again, reappearing as Lependu, a mischief-making, shape-changing figure who undertakes a spiritual quest using local history, shamanic elements, and phrenology to comment upon Western civilization's alienation from its ancestry. Critic Laurie Kruk dubs the long poem a "vocal collage" (49) while Michael Redhill inventively describes it as "a wild roil of lyricism alongside goofball comedy, wordplay and unkempt syntax" (45). Although, unfortunately, out of print, I think *Lependu* is an immensely exciting, vibrant long poem that foregrounds language as subject and structure, form, content, idea, image, and imagination.

McKay's *Lependu* combines poetry and prose; staccato verses alternate with elongated lines flexible as a water dowser's wand that bends and sways to where meaning lies. The poem sequence is a jazzy composite of historical documents merging many voices—including Burley/Lependu's irreverent speech/screech—found material, confessional gleanings, broadsheet, doggerel, Fowler's phrenology lecture, scavenging, alphabetical catalogues of gifts, pictographs, children's word games, drunken grotesquery, comic invention, archeology, dying confessions, tall tales, true confessions, historical plaques, vernacular languages and colloquial speech, shamanic journeyings, cartographic ramblings, invective, free falls into language, an investigation into historic London, Ontario, English and French patois, neologisms, wordplay and punning, onomatopoeia and synaesthesia, guided museum tours offered as a critique of colonization, folksongs, pseudo-scientific taxonomy, and humour (punchline, parody, irony, satire) to deflate pretension.

McKay's poems pull at the semi-permeable membrane between language / laughter and the world in which something, somewhere, always dissolves. A little, a little. In his poem "A Mouth," the speaker watches from a bridge while "some species now extinct" signs to him. In their gestures dwell the motion, the emotion of every creature "as close as / far away" in these pages in these poems, wincing against remembrance:

> every
> feint another beckoning, another
> wave goodbye.
> (*Sanding Down This Rocking Chair*)

On Dogs

> I miss my dog. Together we were purely creature.
> —"Nostra"
> (*Night Field*)

This is the imaginary essay I have not written, but a good place to end or begin, I think: rereading McKay's poems with dogs in mind. Those breathy, brothy, dogged creatures who push their noses into human hands, dash headfirst into trains and headlong through plate glass windows. Who stand up, dazed, and live to wag again. Or don't and swim instead, in the earth, absent-minded as a story that "soon forgets about its dog" ("Running Away," *Another Gravity*) or restless. Restless, yes, as a poem, such as "Loose Ends," in which poetry itself becomes "this white-tipped tail / whose far end was a dog."

One thing that reading Don McKay has taught me is that every ending should be partly imaginary and slightly incomplete. Every end should wag, just a little.

—*Méira Cook*

Bibliography

Primary Sources

McKay, Don. *Air Occupies Space*. Windsor: Sesame Press, 1973.
————. *Long Sault*. (1975). In *The Long Poem Anthology*. Ed. Michael Ondaatje. Toronto: Coach House Press, 1979. 125–57.
————. *Lependu*. Ilderton: Nairn Coldstream, 1978.
————. *Lightning Ball Bait*. Toronto: Coach House Press, 1980.
————. *Birding, or Desire*. Toronto: McClelland and Stewart, 1983.
————. *Sanding Down This Rocking Chair on a Windy Night*. Toronto: McClelland and Stewart, 1987.
————. *Night Field*. Toronto: McClelland and Stewart, 1991.
————. *Apparatus*. Toronto: McClelland and Stewart, 1997.
————. *Another Gravity*. Toronto: McClelland and Stewart, 2000.
————. *Varves*. Edmonton: Extra Virgin Chapbook Press, 2003.
————. *Camber: Selected Poems 1983–2000*. Toronto: McClelland and Stewart, 2004.

Criticism

McKay, Don. "Dot, Line and Circle: A Structural Approach to Dylan Thomas's Imagery." *The Anglo-Welsh Review*. 18.41 (Summer 1969): 69–80.
————. "Aspects of Energy in the Poetry of Dylan Thomas and Sylvia Plath." *Critical Quarterly* 16.1 (Spring 1974): 53–67.
————. "Image of Energy: The Vortex in Dylan Thomas." *English Studies in Canada* 2.3 (Fall 1976): 314–28.
————. "The Impulse to Epic in Goderich, Ontario, or The Huron County Pioneer Museum as a Form of Expression." *Brick* 2 (January 1978): 28–32.
————. "*Long Sault*: Artistic Statement." *The Long Poem Anthology*. Ed. Michael Ondaatje. Toronto: Coach House Press, 1979. 321–22.
————. "Crafty Dylan and the Altarwise Sonnets: 'I build a flying tower and I pull it down.'" *University of Toronto Quarterly* 55.4 (Summer 1986): 375–94.
————. "What Shall We Do with a Drunken Poet? Dylan Thomas's Poetic Language." *Queen's Quarterly* 93.4 (Winter 1986): 794–807.
————. "Local Wilderness" (Editorial). *The Fiddlehead* 169 (Autumn 1991): 5–6.
————. *Vis-à-Vis: Fieldnotes on Poetry and Wilderness*. Wolfville, NS: Gaspereau Press, 2001.

Works Cited

Bondar, Alanna F. "'that every feather is a pen, but living, / flying,' Desire: The Metapoetics of Don McKay's *Birding, or Desire.*" *Studies in Canadian Literature* 19.2 (1994): 14–29.

Bringhurst, Robert. "Unraping the World." Rev. of *Birding, or Desire*, by Don McKay. *Books in Canada* 12.8 (October 1983): 31–32.

Bushell, Kevin. "Don McKay and Metaphor: Stretching Language toward Wilderness." *Studies in Canadian Literature* 21.1 (1996): 37–55.

Coles, Don. "A Gift For Metaphor." Rev. of *Night Field* by Don McKay. *Books in Canada* 20.5 (June/July 1991): 42.

Dragland, Stan. "Be-Wildering: The Poetry of Don McKay." *University of Toronto Quarterly* 70.4 (Fall 2001): 881–88.

———. "A *Long Sault* Primer." *Brick* 3 (Spring 1978): 28–31.

Elmslie, Susan. "'Got to Meander if You Want to Get to Town': Excursion and Excursionist Figures in Don McKay." *Wascana Review* 30.1 (Spring 1995): 77–92.

Forster, Sophia. "Don McKay's Comic Anthropocentrism: Ecocriticism Meets 'Mr. Nature Poet.'" *Essays on Canadian Writing* 77 (Fall 2002): 107–35.

Goulet, Clare. Rev. of *Apparatus* by Don McKay. *Dalhousie Review* 76.2 (Summer 1996): 289–92.

Hopkins, Gerard Manley. *Poems and Prose of Gerard Manley Hopkins*. London: Penguin, 1988.

Kruk, Laurie. "To Scavenge and Invent: The Shamanic Journey in Don McKay's *Lependu.*" *Canadian Poetry* 24 (Spring/Summer 1989): 41–61.

Lilburn, Tim. "How to Be Here?" *Poetry and Knowing: Speculative Essays and Interviews*. Ed. Tim Lilburn. Kingston: Quarry, 1995. 161–76.

Oughton, John. "Lord of the Wings." Rev. of *Sanding Down This Rocking Chair on a Windy Night* by Don McKay. *Books in Canada* 16.5 (June/July 1987): 12–13.

Redhill, Michael. "*Lependu* by Don McKay." *Brick* 61 (Winter 1998): 44–45.

Ruzesky, Jay. Rev. of *Night Field* by Don McKay. *The Malahat Review* 95 (1991): 126.

Down River, Into the Camp

Paddling
establishes, the soft
acceptances of water host us
cradling our cadences, slide
flicker and plunge become
our peristalsis down the river.

Step then into this has-just or
something-about-to-be place, this
demotic am am am among the trees.
Bulldozed into regularity, angrily lit,
        prefabricated someplace else
It is set down here like a spaceship
come to unspell us.

And we are reluctant to leave,
kick empty oil cans, discover a workable
        stove
maybe a mattress? Winches, cable twisting
        off into resurgent scrub,
                                rusted

metal crap,
wind up smoking a cigarette in the bunk-
        house trying to invoke the man
who laid his tired muscles under these
        tits from *Cavalier*
who carved initials in the floor.
But the presences begrudge us.
NE ME BLASPHEME PAS, torn, hangs on the
        wall
like a postcard from someone's forty days.
It's too easy to recall that mosquito whine
magnified, grown to the chain-saw's
        constant drone, more—

carnivorous musak—how many cords,
    how many cords—
Maudite!
Acres of broken brush, browning to tinder,
    and a tidy stack of logs.

The sun pours in as we push off.
Across the river a moose
Warms into shape like a bruise.
Flies surround him, petulant bits of
    the dark.

At the Long Sault Parkway

> 'The noise, the continual motion, and magnitude of the
> contending waves, render the Longue Sault, at once an
> object of terror and delight; these burst upon each other,
> and tossing aloft their broken spray, cover the stream
> with a white and troubled surface, as far as the eye can
> extend.'

And now you're nostalgia, you're a bowl of mushroom soup
tepid and tumid,
teeming with fat carp who feed on your reedy bottom.
But everything's so tasteful, isn't it, so
nice, really, the way they fixed things up with beaches and
everything, and the picnic areas.
No sutures, no Frankenstein bolts through the neck, only
the dam at the end of the lake, a white wink
like a distant TV set
betrays the operation.

You're better off now, rocking on the porch, you lap
lap, lap at the shores of memory,
counting to infinity by ones.
You have old chums here.
These islands are the tops of hills
you used to lash and gnaw.
And here's old Highway 2 who followed you
everywhere.
Always the comic, now he surfaces
to hump an islet
and subside.

I have to go. Rest easy
and so long.

The Great Blue Heron

What I remember
about the Great Blue Heron that rose
like its name over the marsh
is touching and holding that small
manyveined
wrist
upon the gunwale, to signal silently—

                                      look

the Great Blue Heron
(the birdboned wrist).

The Eye Meets Tom Thomson's "A Rapid"

The eye observes the little rapid furl
into the foreground and the yellow
leaves beside it sing right out —
                                        and moves
up river, in, above
the rapid entering
blackness
here at the heart of the canvas.

A backdrop? Yes the eye
sees how the dark sets up
the warbling rapid and the leaves'
five-hundred-watt good-bye.
But also how everything's
imperilled, how Alfred Hitchcock
appears in his own show as a waiter
waiting—
               and moves another step to feel
how textured (are you sure
we're doing the right thing how
depthed it draws us to the pool the pool which
brimsmooth for a stone or for the clean
cleaving a canoe can be the perfect
penis entering an angel, make the shapes appear
in darkness, delicate, dramatic
tangle of twigs or opulent autumn clamouring
paint me paint me as the eye
begins to know each crook and gesture of the long and
infinitely innovative
whorehouse
the velvet
closing as a lid behind.

O scenery's not scenery no more/ the stage
has shifted under us, the show
goes on
and on, beyond all ends
the eye imagines, crazy Wagner,
having killed the gods
again, refusing to finish the banquet, lets
have another sunset pal he turns
to eat the audience—
                    that's you
that's the eye, we'd better
wake up and get out of here friend,
if we can.

The Trout

I   Anger so hot and fine it slides through his brain like silver wire,
flossing back and forth back and forth, establishing a passage
through the continent inside. Not thinking but carrying an infant
thought on the crest of his pain he rides rises on it rushing through
all the boxed in spaces in his head and knocks down walls. Sleep-
walks through the gap in the fence he had been mending, letting
the sledge slide from his grasp, his other hand hanging from his arm
like a dead chicken. And the anger still singing biting out its chapel.
Sleepwalks to the stream where he numbs the smashed hand, his
pure flight wavers and the weak seasickness starts
                And always after knowing
                the hairline fracture his anger can open
                the new sex in his brain

II   At the table
watching their fingers cradle forks like gold pens, flutter
to tuck in strands of hair, curl,
articulate around a glass,
moving like string quintets.
Talking, they build nests in air, the soft
translucence of their knuckles
hurts him.
Feeling his fingers growing into one
dumb fist.

III   What to do with this tired tongue? Ask her how were things
at school ok I guess, the milk cans, the broken
harrow, the mudhole in the lane, the same enumerations—
                he razors from the chair
                and out.

IV   These days his daughter's plainness
sometimes wears a feathery
half-frightened look as a tree in February turning vague
with unseen buds, alive
to its insides

After the slam/ of his exit
she sits in emphatic stillness feeling sick
with richness, eggs and eggs
and eggs she never wanted,
caviar.

V   His daughter stares out the school bus window trying to ignore the
telephone poles flicking like hiccups in her vision. Each day the
same geometry, working out the roads concession by concession,
right angled except where the river forces the road to slither from the
square. There are traps and traps. Her body growing turbid, slow
blood thickening, heavy with dirt. Wishing always to step outside it,
out of bulky winter clothing, thinking of the trout, letting the trout
slide through her thought

slide through her thought pulling its thread of clean and cruel
images, the glint of the ax-blade arcs above his head, glimmerings.
When she gets home she will take an ice-cube from the fridge to
suck, letting it melt in the earth of her.

VI   Drinking wood, drinking the weathered boards
he leans against. The glass
grows to his hand.
The bottle of Dawsons on the chopping block
balanced against the ax.
He waits. His tongue
hovering on his breath.

VII   I feed the chickens, bake for Sunday, dust the parlor we haven't used
it since the minister, weed the kitchen garden. Then I'm free for
picking wild strawberries. I have always liked picking strawberries

since I was a girl. You have to get real close to things to see them, maybe that is why. The closeness. I clomp down the lane in my gumboots, cross the pasture, and through the gap in the fence still unmended, maybe never mended now. Into the rocky field with cedar scrub dotted up and down the slope. A friendly sort of tree. Cross the stream by the plank and up the slope where the straw berries grow thickest, higher the fatter seems to be. They hide their blood-bits close to the ground, you have to hunt for them. I called them blood-bits ever since I was a girl. Blood-bits. I like the sound.

Once I said work is wearing paths on our bodies and they just looked. When I pick strawberries I can feel those paths growing over. I feel like I was taking off gumboots all over my body. Feeling the tickle of the grass blades in my wrist. Feeling the sun's angle in my shoulders. The cloud shadows moving over the ground.

This time I felt another shadow and there was this hawk. He swerved suddenly above the bush, maybe he saw something, and the sun flashed on his underside. I will tell you what it was like. It was like a wild strawberry crushed against the roof of your mouth, a blood-bit.

VIII   At night in the lane he wants to whistle
But the feeling finds no tune   the air
surprising his mouth as a cool breeze
through a fusty old forest.

He aches with his knowing, knowing
it has no tune, there is no way to explain.
He sees his mooncast
shadow move among the other accidents, sees
with an eye cold as the moon
the elm the house the truck the arm the ax

August

Everything is full but she
keeps pumping on the inside
chintzing up the outside till her month becomes
a regular rococco whorehouse in an expanding economy.

Back and forth salaam salaam the sprinklers
graze and pray on plush
carpets of grass, beer becomes sweat, the heavy
air surrounds, mothers us to immobility, the mind
melts, the elements
slump, four fat uncles in their lawn chairs, while the flesh
well the flesh just ambles into town to get drunk with the ball players.

We knew this ripeness and we knew
her smiling, solitary
reaper.
The shiver slid
beneath the sunburn with the fatal
rightness of a shift to minor key:
she loved him, she dressed up in her gypsy best,
she left.

Lependu nearly materialized by his blackbirds

Along the scarecrow's arms & head & shoulders sit
the blackbirds
laughing.

"This is an image of a scarecrow
thinking about blackbirds" they
laugh, thinking of themselves as the thinking
of the scarecrow—ha!
hilarity
fills the air around the scarecrow.

This could almost twist the stitched
mouth into smiling.
To his blackbirds he seems suddenly
bemused.

Field Marks:

just like you and me but
cageless, likes fresh air and
wants to be his longing.
Wears extra eyes around his neck, his mind
pokes out his ears the way an Irish Setter's nose
pokes out a station-wagon window.
His heart is suet. He would be a bird book full of
lavish illustrations with a text of metaphor.
He would know but still
be slippery in time. He would eat crow. He becomes
hyperbole, an egghead who spends days attempting to compare the
shape and texture of her thigh to a snowy egret's neck, elegant
and all too seldom seen in Southern Ontario.
He utters absolutes he instantly forgets. Because
the swallow is intention in a fluid state it is
impossible for it to "miss." On the other
hand a swallow's evening has been usefully compared
to a book comprised entirely of errata slips.

He wings it.

Leaving

The poplars shedding pseudo-suicide notes—
not death but
female impersonation wearing thin,
                                        tra-la.

I crunch them under my tires.

And the sumac,
haunted by her wartime childhood, dreams
how they woke and drove her to the hilltop
to watch the heart of Swansea burning
beautifully
she sets her fires along the roadside.

How am I supposed to drive with these derangements and my head
already full of Monarch Butterflies
massing on Point Pelee,
hanging in their thousands, wings folded
in the wind they look like dun dead leaves themselves their tiny
minds all reaching south in one long
empty line of poetry across the dark waves of Lake Erie?
Wind
stirs some from their branches but
they flutter, flashing orange, and recover
to grip with velvet feet:
                        the concentration of Houdini
                        swells toward his disappearance and return

                in Mexico.

The Boy's Own Guide to Dream Birds

Audubonless
dream birds thrive. The talking swan, the kestrels
nesting in the kitchen, undocumented citizens of teeming
terra incognita.
                 To write
their book the boy will need
la plume de ma tante, harfang des neiges,
patience, an ear like a cornucopia and at least
an elementary understanding of the place of human psychology
among nature's interlocking food chains.
                                For the facts are scarce
and secretive. Who is able to identify
the man in metamorphosis, becoming
half-bird on the Coldstream Road? The boy reports
a falcon's beak both hooked and toothed, the fingers spreading,
lengthening into a vulture's fringe, the cold eye
glaring as he lifts off from the road: look, look,
come quick!
                 Who sits inside and fails to hear?
                 What can he be doing?
                 Why is he so deaf?

But on another night a huge, hunched, crested,
multicoloured bird, a sort of cross between eagle
and macaw, sits, sinister and gorgeous,
on our mailbox.
Now we know what happens to the letters we do not receive
from royalty, and from our secret lovers
pining in the chaste apartments of the waking world.

I Scream You Scream

Waking JESUS sudden riding a scream like a
train braking metal on metal on
metal teeth receiving signals from a dying star sparking
off involuntarily in terror in all directions in the
abstract incognito in my
maidenform bra in an expanding universe in a where's
my syntax thrashing
loose like a grab that like a
look out like a
live wire in a hurricane until

until I finally tie it down:
it is a pig scream
it is a pig scream from the farm across the road
that tears this throat of noise into the otherwise anonymous dark,
a noise not oink or grunt
but a passage blasted through constricted pipes, perhaps
a preview of the pig's last noise.

Gathering again toward sleep I sense
earth's claim on the pig.
Pig grew, polyped out on the earth like a boil
and broke away.
                        But earth
heals all flesh back beginning with her pig,
filling his throat with silt and sending
subtle fingers for him like the meshing fibres in a wound
like roots
like grass growing on a grave like a snooze
in the sun like furlined boots that seize
the feet like his *nostalgie de la boue* like
having another glass of booze like a necktie like a
velvet noose like a nurse

like sleep.

Adagio for a Fallen Sparrow

In the bleak midwinter
frosty wind made moan
earth was hard as iron
water like a stone

Sparrows burning
                        bright bright bright against the wind
resemble this item, this frozen
lump on the floor of my garage, as fire
resembles ash:
                        not much.
A body to dispose of,
probably one I've fed all winter, now
a sort of weightless fact,
an effortless repudiation of the whole shebang.
I'd like to toss it in the garbage can but can't let go
so easily. I'd bury it
but ground is steel
and hard to find. Cremation?
Much too big a deal, too rich and bardic
too much like an ode. Why not simply splurge
and get it stuffed, perch it proudly on the shelf
with Keats and Shelley and *The Birds of Canada*?

But when at last
I bury it beneath three feet of snow
there is nothing to be said.
It's very cold.
The air
has turned its edge
against us.
My bones
are an antenna picking up
arthritis, wordless keening of the dead.

So, sparrow, before drifting snow
reclaims this place for placelessness, I mark your grave
with four sticks broken from the walnut tree:

one for your fierce heart

one for your bright eye

one for the shit you shat upon my windshield
while exercising squatters' rights in my garage

and one to tell the turkey vultures where your thawing body lies
when they return next spring to gather you
into the circling ferment of themselves.

And my last wish: that they do
before the cat discovers you and eats you, throwing up,
as usual, beside the wicker basket in the upstairs hall.

Field Marks (2):

Distinguished from the twerp,
which he resembles, by his off-speed
concentration: *shh*:
                    bursting with sneakiness
he will tiptoe through our early morning drowse
like the villain in an old cartoon, pick up
binoculars, bird book, dog,
orange, letting the fridge lips close behind him with a kiss.
Everything,
even the station-wagon, will be
delicate with dew—
bindweed, spiderweb, sumac,
Queen Anne's Lace: he slides
among them as a wish, attempting to become
a dog's nose of receptiveness.

Later on he'll come back as the well-known bore
and read his list (Song sparrows: 5
                    Brown thrashers: 2
                    Black-throated green warblers: 1)   omitting
all the secret data hatching on the far side of his mind:

                    that birds have sinuses throughout their bodies,
                    and that their bones are flutes
                    that soaring turkey vultures can detect
                                        depression and careless driving
                    that every feather is a pen, but living,

                    flying

Identification

Yesterday a hawkish speck
above the cornfield moving
far too fast its where are those
binoculars sharp wings row row row the air above
the Campbell's bush it
                              stooped and
vanished
                    Peregrine
                              I write it down because

I write it down because of too much sky
because I might have gone on digging the potatoes
never looking up because
I mean to bang this loneliness to speech you
jesus falcon
fix me to my feet and lock me in this
slow sad pocket of awe   because
my sinuses, those weary hoses,
have begun to stretch and grow, become
a catacomb my voice
would yodel into stratospheric octaves
                                        and because
such clarity is rare and inarticulate as you, o dangerous
endangered species.

VIA, Eastbound

To this widescreen three-day tracking shot—equal thirds
of mountain, prairie, boreal forest—
each of us will add a plot:
it is always The Past, but eased,
oiled so it glides and
whispers from its depth, often
with the voice of a lost dog.

Travelling east, we age more quickly,
running into time, which travels
west. This train wants to be evening, wants that
blue grey wash of snow and sky
eliding the horizon,
fading fast.

Toiling through the mountains like the seven
thousand dwarves,
earning every upward inch,
it dreams that the hell of its gut will find release
as lightning.
Everything will lie down in its speed,
a sort of sleep.
Meanwhile each Rocky poses in a sculpted
slow tableau, easily
seducing us to grandeur and glib
notions of eternity.

By nightfall it is chuckling over prairie
running on nothing but the cold air
of Saskatchewan, its dome car
empty as the mind of Buddha.
Window turns to mirror,
a black lake faintly smoked by blowing snow.

In it we can see our ghosts, transparent
creatures of the dark, bravely reading their
reversed editions of the *Calgary Herald*,
riding the freezing wind like gulls.

Buckling

Even the windhover makes mistakes—
some slight
miscalculation and he's prey
to ordinary cats, trailing a slate blue wounded wing
beside the porch. What sort of shrug
suffices? How can we call up Hopkins and
reverse the charges shouting Jesus Christ so
this is fury the whole sky
compressed to microdot   his eye
already fading, no wait as you photograph re
photograph the bird
blooms through your daughter's hand and every
shot will be his absence living in her
finger pen or paintbrush like an empty river, don't
die now: if only he would
sink his hooked beak in your tongue   instead
you feed him stale coke and the
quick lift of caffeine revives him   briefly
sliding a talon through the sweet flesh of your fist

Some Functions of a Leaf

To whisper. To applaud the wind
and hide the Hermit thrush.
To catch the light
and work the humble spell of photosynthesis
(excuse me sir, if I might have one word)
by which it's changed to wood.
To wait
willing to feed
               and be food.

To die with style:
as the tree retreats inside itself,
shutting off the valves at its
extremities
               to starve in technicolour, then
having served two hours in a children's leaf pile, slowly
stir its vitamins into the earth.

To be the artist of mortality.

How to Imagine an Albatross
(assisted by the report of a CIA observer near Christmas Island)

To imagine an albatross
a mind must widen to the breadth of the Pacific Ocean
dissolve its edges to admit a twelve foot wingspan soaring
silently across the soft enormous heave as the planet
breathes into another dawn.
This might be
dream without content or the opening of a film
in which the credits never run no speck appears
on the horizon fattening to Randolph Scott on horseback
     or the lost
brown mole below your shoulder blade, the albatross
is so much of the scene he drinks the ocean never needs
to beat the air into supporting him but
thoughtlessly as an idea, as a phrase-mark holding notes
in sympathy, arcs above the water.

And to imagine an albatross
we must plan to release the rage
which holds this pencil in itself, to prod things
until their atoms shift, rebel against their thingness, chairs
run into walls, stones
pour like a mob from their solidity.

A warm-up exercise:
                         once
in London, Ontario, a backhoe accidentally
took out a regulator on the gas-line, so the pressure
     of the system
rushed the neighbourhood. Stoves
turned into dragons and expressed
their secret passions all along the ordinary street
the houses bloomed fiercely as the peonies in their front
     yards.

Meanwhile the albatross, thoughtlessly
as an idea, as a phrase-mark holding notes
in sympathy, arcs into a day
that will escape the dull routine of dayness and achieve
crescendo.
                              Placing ourselves safely
at a distance we observe
how the sky burns off its blueness to unveil
the gaze of outer space, which even here
has turned the air psychotic. The birds
start smoking, then,
as though Van Gogh were painting them, turn
cartwheels in the air, catch fire
and fall into the ocean.
What saves us now from heat and light
what keeps us now from biting off our tongues
what stops blood boiling through the heart blocks
recognition of this burning curve
slicing like a scythe through the mind
is what hereafter will protect us

from the earth.

from Black Spruce

Along the shoreline, shelves, soft
curves as the rock
erotically enters water. Shoulder
knuckle skull hip vertebreast combined and
recombined: three
hundred million years before the animals
appeared in the Triassic
they were dreamt of in Precambrian
volcanoes. Feel the muscle
slide over bone as you crouch
beside a Harebell, think of rootlets
reaching into rock, licking its slow
fury into food,
hoisting this small blue flag.

Another Theory of Dusk

What is there to say
when the sky pours in the window
and the ground begins to eat its figures?
We sit like dummies in our kitchen, deaf
among enormous crumplings of light.
Small wonder each thing looms
crowding its edge.
In silent movies everyone overacts a little.

It would be nice to breathe the air inside the cello.
That would satisfy one
thirst of the voice. As it is

only your ribcage speaks for me now,
a wicker basket full of sorrow and wish, so tough
so finely tuned we have often
reinvented the canoe

and paddled off.
It would be nice to write the field guide for those riverbanks,
to speak without names of the fugitive
nocturnal creatures that live and die in our lives.

Meditation on a Geode

To find one, even among souvenirs of Banff from acrylic to zinc, is to realize that rock, ordinary limestone, composes in its own medium and has other lives. This one sits by the telephone, an impacted hollow whole note, formed, says my old geology textbook, from the modification and enlargement of an original void. O : every time I look inside, that twinge of tabu. And something more familiar: impossible words forming a lump in my throat, the petrified ovary of the unspoken.

I have been trying to respond to the spaces in your letter, its rests and lapses, and the slight halo effect of words spoken in an art gallery. Thanks especially for the potato salad recipe with the missing mystery ingredient. You've been breathing the spiked air of solitude and I'm feeling jealous. Echoless. Probably I should get more exercise, once upon a time, once upon a time. Meanwhile the geode by the phone. Astounded.

Once upon a time there was a little animal who lived and died, got buried in the silt and gradually decayed to nothing, which filled up with water. And on the inner surface of the hole a shell of jellied silica dividing the water inside, which is quite salty, from the fresher water outside in the limestone: a tiny ocean in an egg. In which a subtle and irresistible idea, osmosis, unclenches outward against the rock, widening the hole and seeping through the silica until the salts inside and outside balance. And everything (slow gong) crystallizes: : animal, emptiness, ocean, gland : ode of the earth.

Choosing the Bow

In the factory of lever and hinge
all poems begin with oil

•

Medicine stick, belly of earth, medicine stick, belly of earth

•

That an impulse travels shoulder-elbow-wrist and gathers
(sensory redundance) in the fingertips has generally been
assumed. Recently, however, the discovery of the dendritic
aureole (the "moustache" or otter-awareness effect) has given
rise to speculation that the fiddler experiences vestigial antennae
like the phantom pain of amputated limbs and that her
experience of muscular *déjà vu* is, as it were, thousands of absent
sensilla placodea grieving for themselves.

•

The dark bow, you explain, wants her head and
flicks into saltando, taking arpeggia
the way a teenager takes stairs. The heavier,
reddish bow will bite and makes a crosshatched,
comfortable largo. In the kitchen
the violin-maker's daughter is pretending
she has lost her hands.
Where did they go?
Are they hiding under the snow, clasped,
plotting in their sleep like rhizomes?
Before the discovery of America,
her father says, bows were made of ironwood.
Now we use pernambuco, from Brazil,
a wood so dense it
tenses at the slightest flex
and sinks in water. Outside the window, snow
swoons abundantly into its soft self, as though
a great composer had stopped

dead in his tracks, spilling an infinity of crotchets
quavers phrases into the earth's lap.

You guess where did my hands go, o.k.?
Have they moved in
with the rabbits, to stroke their terrors
and teach them to count?
Or are they stealing secrets
from the spruce, the horse, the pernambuco,
maple, whale, ebony, elephant and cat
in order to compose themselves a voice?

Riversinew forming in the other room.

Someone knocking at the door.

Meditation on Shovels

How well they love us, palm and instep, lifeline
running with the grain as we
stab   pry   heave
our grunts and curses are their music.
What a (stab) fucking life, you dig these
(pry) dumb holes in the ground and (heave) fill
them up again until they (stab)
dig a fucking hole for you:
                              beautiful,
they love it, hum it as they stand,
disembodied backbones,
waiting for you to get back to work.

But in the Book of Symbols, after Shoes
(Van Gogh, Heidegger, and Cinderella)
they do not appear.
Of course not.
                    They're still out there
humming
patiently pointing down.

Poplar

Speak gently of Poplar, who has
incompletely metamorphosed out of flesh
and still recalls the Saturday night
bath and toughly tender country blues which,
when she used to travel,
moved her.
Consider that her leaves are hearts,
sharpened and
inverted into spades. Who else
has strength to tremble,
tremble and be wholly trepid,
to be soft so she can listen hard,
and shimmer, elegant and humble,
in the merest wisp of wind?
Who blurs the brittle
creek bank, lisping into spring?
Who feeds the beaver, living in their culture
as potato lives in Irish? Well,
if a man begin to wonder in his tracks and
at them, arrowing behind him and before, should purpose
slow, grow empty arms,
and know itself again as slough or delta, then
that sometime man may wish for a chair of
                          comprehending wood
to lay his many bones in: Poplar.

Early Instruments

The wolf at the door
and the wolf in the forest and the work
work work of art. The scrape,
the chop, the saw tooth
tasting maple. The cradle, the cup, the muscle
in your mother's arm and back
and pelvis, muscle flexing in the air
between two people arguing,
two people loving, muscle
pumping blood. Gut
summoned to speak. The rotary cuff, the wrist,
having learnt the trick of witching wands and locks,
the heft, the grain, the web,
the rub of moving parts.
And the tiny sea in the ear
and the moth wing in the mind, which wait.

Twinflower

What do you call
the muscle we long with? Spirit?
I don't think so. Spirit is a far cry. This
is a casting outward which
unwinds inside the chest. A hole
which complements the heart.
The ghost of a chance.

*

Then God said, ok let's get this show
on the road, boy, get some names
stuck on these critters, and Adam,
his head on the ground in a patch of tiny
pink-white flowers, said
mmn, just a sec.
He was, let's say,
engrossed in their gesture,
the two stalks rising, branching, falling back
into nodding bells, the fading arc
that would entrance Pre-Raphaelites and basketball.
Maybe he browsed among the possibilities of elves.
Maybe he was blowing on the blossoms,
whispering whatever came into his head, I have
no way of knowing what transpired
as Adam paused, testing his parent's
limit, but I know
it matters.

*

Through the cool woods of the lower
slopes, where the tall
Lodgepole Pine point
into the wild blue while they supervise
the shaded space below, I walk,

accompanied by my binoculars and field guides.
I am working on the same old problem,
how to be both
knife and spoon, when there they are, and maybe have been
all along, covering the forest floor: a creeper, a shy
hoister of flags, a tiny lamp to read by, one
word at a time.

           Of course, having found them, I'm about
to find them in the field guide, and the bright
reticulated snaps of system will occur
as the plant is placed, so, among the honeysuckles,
in cool dry northern woods from June to August.
But this is not, despite the note of certainty,
the end. Hold the book open,
leaf to leaf. Listen now,
Linnaea Borealis, while I read of how
you have been loved—
with keys and adjectives and numbers, all the teeth
the mind can muster. How your namer,
Carolus Linnaeus, gave you his
to live by in the system he devised.
How later, it was you,
of all the plants he knew and named,
he asked to join him in his portrait.
To rise in your tininess,
to branch and nod beside him
as he placed himself in that important
airless room.

Alibi

Because the swallows had departed from the cliff,
over and over,
the soft knives of their wings tasting the river mist as they
went wherever it is
they went, because
with the air free of their chatter we could hear ourselves
think, because the notes
we left in their holes, full of love and envy
and lament, were never answered and because we need
an earth with ears to hear the long dread
carpentry of history, and then, and so, and so,
and then, each bone nailed, wired, welded,
riveted, because we knew
the gods we loved were charismatic fictions, and because
the swallows had departed.

Matériel

(i) The Man from Nod

Since his later history is so obscure, it's no wonder he is most remembered for his first bold steps in the areas of sibling rivalry and land use. It should not be forgotten that, although Adam received God's breath, and angels delivered his message, it was Cain who got tattooed—inscribed with the sign which guarantees a sevenfold revenge to be dished out to antagonists. Sometimes translated "Born to Lose."

He was the first to realize there is no future in farming.

How must he have felt, after tilling, sowing, weeding, harvesting, and finally offering his crop, about God's preference for meat? Was God trying to push his prized human creatures further into the fanged romance of chasing and escaping? Was he already in the pocket of the cattle barons? Cain must have scratched and scratched his head before he bashed in his brother's.

He becomes the first displaced person, exiled to the land of Nod, whose etymology, as he probably realized, was already infected with wandering. Then his biography goes underground, rumouring everywhere. Some say he tries farming once again in the hinterland, scratching illegibly at the glacial till before hitting the first road. Some say he fathers a particularly warlike tribe, the Kenites. Some, like Saint Augustine, claim that he takes revenge on agriculture by founding the first cities, rationalizing all his wanderings into streets and tenements, and so charting the course for enclosures and clearances to come. But perhaps his strategy is simpler and more elegant. Perhaps he just thins into his anger, living as a virus in the body politic: the wronged assassin, the antifarmer, the terrorist tattooed with the promise of sevenfold revenge. Like anyone, he wants to leave his mark.

(ii) Fates Worse Than Death

Atrocity
implies an audience of gods.
The gods watched as swiftfooted
godlike Achilles cut behind the tendons of both feet
and pulled a strap of oxhide through
so he could drag the body of Hektor,
tamer of horses, head down in the dust
behind his chariot.
Some were appalled, some not,
having nursed their grudges well, until
those grudges were fine milkfed
adolescents, armed
with automatic weapons. The gods,
and farther off,
the gods before the gods, those who ate
their children and contrived
exquisite tortures in eternity, watched
and knew themselves undead. Such is the loss, such
the wrath of swiftfooted godlike
Achilles, the dumb fucker, that he drags,
up and down, and round and round the tomb
of his beloved, the body of Hektor,
tamer of horses. Atrocity
is never senseless. No. Atrocity is dead ones
locked in sense, forbidden
to return to dust, but scribbled in it,
so that everyone—the gods,
the gods before the gods, the enemy, the absent mothers, all
must read what it is like to live out exile on the earth
without it, to be without recesses, place,
a campsite where the river opens
into the lake, must read
what it means to live against the sun and not to die.
Watch,
he says, alone in the public

newscast of his torment, as he
cuts behind the tendons of both feet,
and pulls a strap of oxhide through,
so he can drag the body that cannot stop being Hektor,
tamer of horses, head down in the dust
behind his chariot, watch
this.

Setting the Table

(i) Knife

who comes to the table fresh
from killing the pig, edge
of edges,
entry into zip.
                    Knife
who can swim as its secret
through the dialogue or glimmer
in a kitchen drawer. Who first appeared
in God's hand to divide
the day from the night, then the sheep
from the goats, then from the other
sheep, then from their comfortable
fleeces. Nothing sinister in this except
it had to happen and it was the first
to have to. The imperative
mood. For what we are about to take
we must be grateful.

(ii) Fork

a touch of kestrel,
of Chopin, your hand with its fork
hovers above the plate, or punctuates
a proposition. This is the devil's favourite
instrument, the fourfold
family of prongs: Hard Place,
Rock, Something You Should Know,
and For Your Own Good. At rest,
face up, it says,
please, its tines
pathetic as an old man's fingers on a bed.
Face down it says
anything that moves.

(iii) Spoon

whose eloquence
is tongueless, witless, fingerless,
an absent egg.
Hi Ho, sing knife and fork, as off they go,
chummy as good cop and bad cop,
to interrogate the supper. Spoon waits
and reflects your expression,
inverted, in its tarnished moonlight. It knows
what it knows. It knows hunger
from the inside
out.

Sometimes a Voice (1)

Sometimes a voice—have you heard this?—
wants not to be voice any longer, wants something
whispering between the words, some
rumour of its former life. Sometimes, even
in the midst of making sense or conversation, it will
hearken back to breath, or even farther,
to the wind, and recognize itself
as troubled air, a flight path still
looking for its bird.
                  I'm thinking of us up there
shingling the boathouse roof. That job is all
off balance—squat, hammer, body skewed
against the incline, heft the bundle,
daub the tar, squat. Talking,
as we have always talked, about not living
past the age of thirty with its
labyrinthine perils: getting hooked,
steady job, kids, business suit. Fuck that. The roof
sloped upward like a take-off ramp
waiting for Evel Knievel, pointing into open sky. Beyond it
twenty feet or so of concrete wharf before
the blue-black water of the lake. Danny said
that he could make it, easy. We said
never. He said case of beer, put up
or shut up. We said
asshole. Frank said first he should go get our beer
because he wasn't going to get it paralysed or dead.
Everybody got up, taking this excuse
to stretch and smoke and pace the roof
from eaves to peak, discussing gravity
and Steve McQueen, who never used a stunt man, Danny's
life expectancy, and whether that should be a case
of Export or O'Keefe's. We knew what this was—

ongoing argument to fray
the tedium of work akin to filter vs. plain,
stick shift vs. automatic, condom vs.
pulling out in time. We flicked our butts toward the lake
and got back to the job. And then, amid the squat,
hammer, heft, no one saw him go. Suddenly he
wasn't there, just his boots
with his hammer stuck inside one like a heavy-headed
flower. Back then it was bizarre that,
after all that banter, he should be so silent,
so inward with it just to
run off into sky. Later I thought,
cool. Still later I think it makes sense his voice should
sink back into breath and breath
devote itself to taking in whatever air
might have to say on that short flight between the roof
and the rest of his natural life.

Load

We think this
the fate of mammals—to bear, be born,
be burden, to carry our own bones
as far as we can and know the force that earths us
intimately. Sometimes, while I was reading,
Sam would bestow one large paw on my foot,
as if to support my body
while its mind was absent—mute
commiseration, load to load, a message
like the velvet heaviness which comes
to carry you deliciously
asleep.
　　　　One morning
on the beach at Point Pelee, I met
a White-throated Sparrow so exhausted from the flight
across Lake Erie it just huddled in itself
as I crouched a few yards off.
I was thinking of the muscles in that grey-white breast,
pectoralis major powering each downstroke,
pectoralis minor with its rope-and-pulley tendon
reaching through the shoulder to the
top side of the humerus to haul it up again;
of the sternum with the extra keel it has evolved to
anchor all that effort, of the dark wind
and the white curl on the waves below, the slow dawn
and the thickening shoreline.
　　　　　　　　　I wanted
very much to stroke it, and recalling
several terrors of my brief
and trivial existence, didn't.

Luna Moth Meditation

How foolish to think death's pale flag
would be rectangular and stark, rather than this
scrap of wedding dress symmetrically ripped
and sent back, cruelly,
to be his deaf and nearly mouthless
messenger. As it unfolds—gorgeous, appalling—
I can feel my mind fill up
with its own weight, as though
suffering unexpected snowfall.
Think of a Eurydice who makes it
all the way, following an Orpheus
with more self-discipline,
and probably less talent, just to find herself
forbidden that huge
other eros:
                    how she craves the darkness and her legs
drink down into dirt. And that moment
in the sickroom when the dead one's been removed
and the Kleenex in the waste can
starts to metamorphose, tissue
taking wing, wing
taking the very drape and slope of grief
and struggling out the door.

Hush Factor

Rogue translation. Out of lullaby and slow
cathedral air to wrench this barely
thickened sibilance and make it mean
the sudden death of sound: *hush.*
                                    So more
than silent is the flight of owls
the slightest rustle gives itself away,
conspires to perish.
The owls have struck a deal with drag, their wide wings
fringed like petticoats, the underneath
covered by a sort of nap as though
wearing frillies on the outside.
They come as a quilt,
as the softness inside touch that
whispers in your skin.
The neighbourhoods they flow through
turn into the underworld unfolding behind Orpheus as,
endlessly, he climbs toward us—the deep call
of its gravity, the frail memory of day,
the vertigo which is the cocktail of the two together
mixing in his mind: *hush.*
                          The Barred Owl swept
out of our neighbour's tree and passed
just above our heads before it vanished
into the yard across the street. And awe rose,
from what depth we could not say, and left the dusk
seduced. We turned to walk back home. What cats,
we wondered, were just then being let out,
lovingly, into the night?

Sometimes a Voice (2)

Sometimes a voice—have you heard this?—
wants not to be voice any longer and this longing
is the worst of longings. Nothing
assuages. Not the curry-comb of conversation,
not the dog-eared broken
satisfactions of the blues. It huddles in the lungs
and won't come out. Nor for the Mendelssohn Choir
constructing habitable spaces in the air, not for Yeats
intoning "Song of the Old Mother" to an ancient
microphone. It curls up in its cave
and will not stir. Not for the gentle quack
of saxophone, not for raven's far-calling
croak. Not for *oh* the lift of poetry, or *ah*
the lover's sigh, or *um* the phrase's lost
left shoe. It tucks its nose beneath its brush
and won't. If her whisper tries
to pollinate your name, if a stranger yells
hey kid, va t'en chez toi to set another music
going in your head it simply
enters deafness. Nothing
assuages. Maybe it is singing
high in the cirque, burnishing itself
against the rockwall, maybe it is
clicking in the stones turned by the waves like faceless
dice. Have you heard this?—in the hush
of invisible feathers as they urge the dark,
stroking it toward articulation? Or the moment
when you know it's over and the nothing which you
have to say is falling all around you, lavishly,
pouring its heart out.

Astonished—

       astounded, astonied, astunned, stopped short
       and turned toward stone, the moment
       filling with its slow
       stratified time. Standing there, your face
       cratered by its gawk,
       you might be the symbol signifying æon.
       What are you, empty or pregnant? Somewhere
       sediments accumulate on seabeds, seabeds
       rear up into mountains, ammonites
       fossilize into gems. Are you thinking
       or being thought? Cities
       as sand dunes, epics
       as e-mail. Astonished
       you are famous and anonymous, the border
       washed out by so soft a thing as weather. Someone
       inside you steps from the forest and across the beach
       toward the nameless all-dissolving ocean.

Afterword

The Shell of the Tortoise

To write about my own writing: this could be perilous. Just contemplating it from a distance, I can feel the threat of conjecture stiffening toward rhetoric, the shadow of a quasi-official practice falling across my loose collection of habits and tricks. So what I need to do first is to invoke a protective presence, a companion who can be depended upon to prevent seriousness from deviating into solemnity, who will cast a wry destabilizing smile on any reflections that show signs of hardening into plaques. I need to ask Hermes to keep an eye on things.

The lyre—the poet's instrument—belongs first to Apollo, and then to Orpheus. But the god who *invents* it, over and over, is Hermes. Trickster, messenger of the gods, cattle rustler, psychopomp, Hermes is the invaluable guide and companion to all mortals making perilous crossings—between mortal and divine realms, between antagonistic neighbourhoods within the self, between the lands of the living and the dead. Between-ness, *metoxa*, might be called the country of Hermes, although of course it is really the absence of country; it is passage, threshold, transition. It is a paradoxical truth, which people in difficult transit often come to appreciate, that in the throes of transformation, when our usual benchmarks and compass readings are awry, we come to trust the trickster, the only figure at home in these conditions. For me it is important that Hermes, and not the sun-god Apollo or the peerless artist Orpheus invents the instrument of poetry, since I experience poetic composition as just such an uncertain passage.

Here's the story. Very soon after he was born, Hermes performed two symbolic acts: he stole the cattle owned by his esteemed brother, Apollo, and he invented the lyre. The latter involved (and involves, since stories like this occur in a kind of atemporal present) combining a pure perception—a flash of inspiration—with the ingenious exercise of craft. The inspiration came when Hermes spotted a tortoise outside the city gate and immediately saw that this "shapely hoofer" could become "the companion of the feast"—an epithet attached by Homer to the lyre, signalling that Hermes not only foresaw the instrument but the heroic tradition of poetic storytelling. The crafty part involved killing the tortoise, then hollowing out the shell to make a resonating chamber (the nothing that speaks, as it is said), attaching reeds from the river to make the neck and crosspiece, fixing sheep gut in place for the strings, and covering the whole contraption with oxhide—taken, of course, from those rustled cattle. Craft, as the word's rich range of meaning implies, is where art and cunning come together.

In the Homeric hymn to Hermes where we find this story, it can be said that he is presented not only as the inventor of the lyre but as the inventor of invention. Notice how the hymn takes time to focus on him at the point most appropriate to his character, in the middle of the creative process:

> As when swift thought pierces the breast
> of a man in whom thick-coming cares churn,
> or when flashes glance from quick-rolling eyes,
> so glorious Hermes pondered word and deed at once.

Some of us, holding this figure in our minds' eyes, may recognize him: an uncle, a neighbour, maybe your grandfather, standing by his workbench holding an unlikely, probably pronged, piece of equipment picked up at a yard sale or Canadian Tire, pondering. He is on the threshold of an invention that will either revolutionize wood-splitting forever (his version) or maim the investor and any unlucky spectators who happen by (your grandmother). The inventor of the lyre is a *bricoleur*, brilliant and ruthless; he uses what comes to hand, connecting the tortoise with the contraband oxhide he just happens to have handy, grading reeds from the river and guts from the sheep. Nor does he pause long over trifles like whether the tortoise, ox, or sheep would prefer to carry on as living animals rather than contribute to the divine instrument. The fit of invention is upon him.

As I make this gesture of homage and invocation, it is important for me also to observe what a composite character this creator is, pondering "word and deed at once." No pure Orphic lyricist, or empty-headed mystic, Hermes is as much a creation of *bricolage* as the contraption he's cobbling together. I love the hymn's take on the creative moment—"as when swift thought pierces the breast / of a man in whom thick-coming cares churn": exactly. We know how this works. Your landlord has sent the final notice for the overdue rent; your roommate has brought home a gerbil that runs all night on its exercise wheel; you have mono and a hangover. Now inspiration, a "swift thought" pierces your breast. There is some connection, let's say, between the way a dipper casually steps into turbulence and a John Coltrane entry, and both prickle away at your intuition, a pre-echo of some fresh wisdom, like a sneeze approaching from a distance. Do you attend to those thick-coming cares or let them churn away by themselves while you pick up your pencil? No need to pause long over *that* question, or waste time while you explain yet again that pencils have been rendered obsolete by laptops. What's interesting here is how, at the level of the origins of the art, those day-to-day cares are acknowledged, as well as inspiration's uncanny knack of striking at the least opportune moment. Invoking Hermes the lyre-maker is a way to remind ourselves that art grows in uncertainty, in trouble, in the coming-together of unlikely combinations, as it makes its rash and violent translation from raw materials to instrument.

And it occurs to me that the conclusion of the story may hold lessons for me at this particular threshold. Why should Apollo wind up with the lyre, and be thereafter acclaimed the god of music, if Hermes invented it and, according to the hymn, played it beautifully? We go back to the original theft of Apollo's cattle, and the sun god's extensive network of associations and spies. Eventually Hermes (he's still just a kid, really) gets tracked down by his brother and accused of the crime. In the midst of their confrontation, the lyre, this "lovely toy," is brought from its hiding place and offered in trade for Apollo's dropping the charges. Of course Apollo immediately recognizes the value of the instrument, accepts the plea bargain, and even offers to let Hermes keep the remaining cattle as part of the deal. Our attention might reasonably shift to the sun god here, and the glorious musical and poetic feats accomplished under his patronage, but let's stick with Hermes. Does he scheme to get the lyre back? Does he bear a grudge? Hermes simply turns his talents—disruptive, companionable, risky—elsewhere. The hermetic artist does this most difficult thing: she walks away from the products of her art. As the *Tao te Ching* has it, she does her work, and steps back; she does not cling to her creations. But what about reputation, awards, fame, representation in anthologies? What about (you are perhaps already asking this) perpetrating an essay, or proto-essay, about her own inventions?

Nevertheless, I said I would say something and now, having performed a gesture of propitiation, I should get on with it. So let me hazard a brave claim, and see where it takes us. "Art occurs whenever a tool attempts to metamorphose into an animal." As you can see, this connects with the story of Hermes' lyre, whose music is the singing of the tortoise.

Of course, a musical instrument is a special kind of tool, one that remembers its link to daemonic energies outside the human sphere. But what my brave claim implies is that tool use itself, the very faculty that enables us to successfully domesticate the world, harbours this illicit desire for wildness. In so many ways, tools define us: a person without tools is, in our thinking, poor, a bare forked animal like Poor Tom in *King Lear*, at risk of slipping below the ranks of the human. At the other end of the economic spectrum, we frequently measure well-being and wealth by the number and sophistication of the tools we own, and how far they extend beyond raw need (Poor Tom could use a blanket) into luxury (your laptop, my self-defrosting fridge). Indeed, tools are so intimately worked into the fabric of life that it becomes a question of who uses whom. Thinkers as diverse as William Blake, Eric Gill, J.L. Livingstone, and Marshall McLuhan have observed that our dependency runs so deep that the tools may be said to operate us, that we have, as Livingstone puts it, domesticated ourselves to technology. When the tail has wagged the dog long enough, it gets to be the dog.

The brave claim is that we can see art as a subversion of that process, indeed as a counter-flow. Inside tool use, inside the ethos of domestication, this illicit, delicious desire emerges, this urge to connect with the world in a way that lets primal otherness loose inside culture. The tool discovers that its being is not entirely used up in utility; it yearns toward the animal. Of course I am not suggesting that it actually succeeds in going wild. The paint in Van Gogh's *Stormy Night* remains paint, like the paint on the walls of your house; the stone in the statue remains a cultural artefact, like the stone in its foundations; the piece of Sitka spruce used to make the top of the guitar is just as "instrumental" as the pieces used to build airplanes. But in all cases you can feel that longing, that quiver of imminent metamorphosis, in the vibrant aesthetic pause they create, in the arresting moment of art. I think the outward evidence of this desire is that the tool seems less of a tool, and more of a medium. That is, it slides toward the message-bearing, border-crossing function we associate with Hermes.

So, what about poetry? As with painting, sculpture, and music, poetry is the reanimation of a tool, but, since language is the powerful and mysterious medium that it is, its case is more problematic. What is this language thing, anyway? A supertool? A modality of being? A fifth dimension? It is clear that it stands in a special relation to us as human beings: it empowers us in our organization of the world; it enables us to render things symbolically, and to manipulate the symbols; it allows us the freedom to speculate, as I am so lavishly doing here. But—so says the brave claim—language, too, nurtures that secret animal dream, a dream often expressed in the negative as doubt about its own organizing and manipulative activities. When it acts on these urges and doubts, the effect can be like seeing a fish suddenly surface in a canal—a troubling of the waters, a surge of eros, as flash, a leap.

> Terrifying are the attent sleek thrushes on the lawn,
> More coiled steel than living—a poised
> Dark deadly eye, those delicate legs

Triggered to stirrings beyond sense—with a start, a bounce, a stab
Overtake the instant and drag out some writhing thing
—Ted Hughes, "Thrushes"

There is something uncanny about this, something that slips across bound-
aries, something subversive, some secret revealing its energies. "Attent sleek
thrushes"; Hermes is present here, certainly as trickster, hopefully as guide,
when language gestures to this terror, re-introducing wilderness both to the
lawn, with its invisible writhing lives, and to the thrushes, whose songs have
been elevated to near-angelic status in romantic poems, now re-seen as killers.
This energy discharge is dangerous the way all occurrences of wilderness are
dangerous—not because it wishes us harm, but because it represents a potency
beyond our control. Language is surprised, shocked, by those volts inside
itself, even though it has contrived the event. The medium we use all the time
to keep our lives going, in which we chat, gossip, plan, and argue, responds to
both its deep erotic urge and its suspicion of its own inadequacy. Here's how
Elias Canetti responds to what is probably our most necessary and cliché-
damaged words. "To find a stronger word for love, a word that would be like
wind, but from under the earth, a word that doesn't need mountains, but
enormous caves in which it houses." The chthonic word; the wind from the
earth: here language is longing for "stirrings beyond sense," for animal
presence, the voice that would serve to connect us with the earth. Oracle,
in short.

•

Re-enter Hermes. What I've said is clearly too abstract, too coyly wise. In
practice a poet fumbles about, rummages (remember your grandfather in his
workshop), having been smitten by a frisson or hunch, trying to get a handle
on it by listening through language. What a critic or teacher would call tech-
niques (various structures, rhythm, rhyme, and other musical connections,
metaphorical reaches) seem to me, mid-rummage, to be more like sensors,
listening devices like radio telescopes or sonar. It's as though language, which
is—so we think—all mouth, were trying to grow ears.

For instance: I am sitting in a house once owned by one of the world's
greatest fishermen and lovers of rivers, Roderick Haig-Brown, situated on the
banks of the Campbell River on Vancouver Island. The river is sliding past the
window, sleek, slate-coloured, muscular, and here I am once again in the grip
of Herakleitos, philosopher of flux, imagining inside that current the potent
counter-rhythm created by the upstream surge of the Chum and Coho salmon
intent on reaching their spawning redds in the Campbell, the Quinsam, or
their tributary creeks. I'm wondering about various listening devices I might

send out: long-lived dithyrambic celebrations; or maybe blank verse would convey the weight of it, the gravitas; or maybe quick imagistic takes with lots of silences through which the flow might move. Right now I'm wondering about using a prose line (probably I'm inspired by those line loops and curves cast by the fly fishermen just upstream), something to pick up on its ceaselessness, a line that might be induced to modify its syntax, maybe open doors at both ends in order to attend to this urgent counterpointed energy. (Aside to Herakleitos: I see your point about no man stepping twice into the same river, but I've a feeling it doesn't apply to salmon.) In my cluttered workshop, the prose line is a handy device, since it can often supply details overlooked by poetry. Sent out on reconnaissance, the poetic line really does act like a bird, winging perch to perch, image to image, berry to berry. The prose line behaves more like a dog—footed, tactless, indentured to its nose, in love with the neighbour's garbage. The sweet stench of the Coho rotting along the bank might be just its thing.

If one of these listening devices brings back something helpful to the hunch, it will arrive like the "swift thought" that pierced Hermes' breast with its thick-coming cares. (Well, a scaled-down version of that event: we're talking about yet another take on the salmon cycle here, not the invention of the lyre itself.) That might trigger other thoughts, or images, or scraps of music, and one day—a day I can only hope for, not believe in—those might find themselves cohering as a poem. There is another magic in that coming-together, since it often seems that the bits achieve this by conversing—"jamming" is a better word for it—with each other. Always cacophonously at first, with me sitting on the sidelines, occasionally prodding, coaxing, arranging. I think of Jimmy Rabbit in *The Commitments*, with his unruly band. Sometimes I think herding cats would be easier.

This prompts me to say something about form, a tricky subject, especially since I do not identify it with those marvelous prosodic structures (sonnet, terza rima, glosas, pantoums, *cyghannedd*) which have collected in the multi-cultural ragbag of the English tradition. Instead of venturing a further brave claim, let me call again upon Herakleitos. One of his fragments is *harmoniē aphanē phaneres kreitton*: translated by Charles Kahn as "The hidden attunement is better than the obvious one." I think that the poet, rummaging in that workshop, or listening with dismay to the crashings of her proto-band, has an ear out for such deep harmony, such hidden attunement. But notice also that the fragment demonstrates, in its extraordinary music, how a surface harmony may resonate with a deep one, like an unforgettable chord. The form of a work is something it discovers, its *telos*, not its starting point, and I often feel a scruple—or it may be a superstition—about discussing it. It's as though deep form were a fugitive species thriving in concealment, properly addressed by chaste gestures rather than definitions. "Drawing is not form," says Degas, "it is the way you see form." Needless to say, I am out of sympathy with the institutionalization of form as an "ism," a sort of taxidermy which has occurred, or reoccurred, recently.

•

I have spoken much about this tool, the lyre made from murdered animals, and not much about the animals themselves. Let me go back to that story for a moment. There is a bracing candour to the violence of Hermes, who, though ruthless, is in no doubt about the debt he owes the tortoise. But something happens as the lyre is passed on, a combination of forgetfulness and hubris, or overweening pride. By the time it has been traded to Apollo, then passed down to Orpheus, the myth of the artist is in full cry. The art of Orpheus, it is said, enchants animals, makes rocks move and induces trees to dance. But— if we recall Hermes the lyre-maker—it was the very dynamism of the natural world that animated the lyre in the first place. This is equivalent to a cook taking credit for the sweetness of the plum and the bitterness of the lemon. It might also be useful to reflect that, in fact, rocks do move on their own in the constant remaking of the planet; that only a small effort of imagination is needed to perceive the dance of trees; and that no one, in the presence of a wild salmon or thrush can be in any doubt about who is enchanting whom. We find such forgetfulness and hubris in romanticism at the point where the reality of the world is taken to depend on the creativity of the arts, and in Heidegger at the point where Being is made to depend on language for its articulation. Who do we think we are, as artists? It's a question worth posing repeatedly, akin to asking, in the supermarket, where the food comes from. If our answer is that we are co-creators of reality, or shepherds of being, then I think we need to remind ourselves of the tortoise and its shell. Orpheus, it is worth remembering, wound up getting torn apart by the Maenads as punishment for his failure to properly acknowledge Dionysos, the god of natural energies.

My own hubris, with respect to natural presence, has its roots deep in a misspent youth. It's not that I didn't spend much of it in the wilderness; in fact many summers were passed paddling the lakes and rivers of the Precambrian Shield. It's just that I wasn't paying attention. We travelled through this amazing country in a spirit akin to tourists who do the Louvre in an afternoon. "We covered 250 miles in five days": could that have been true? It's certainly true that few organisms smaller than moose managed to penetrate the thick hide of our inattention.

So, if there is an afterlife, one in which rewards are dished out, like Air Miles prizes for good behaviour, and if (Big If) I manage to accumulate enough points for some of those Bonus Return packages, I will cash them all in and repaddle the Camachigama, the Upper Ottawa, the Diable, the Goulais (all in pristine condition, of course), giving full attention to birds, animals, plants, and lichens, not to mention the eloquent, glacier-inscribed granite itself. Among my companions on these trips (perhaps substituting for one another, like players during all-star games) I will find Basho, Black Elk, Rachel Carson, Stephen Jay Gould, David Suzuki, Margaret Avision, and Roderick Haig-Brown. Herakleitos and Parmenides will paddle in one canoe, taking turns in the stern, so that the river is sometimes the same, sometimes not. And the guide? But you have already guessed the identity of that figure, with his nondescript grey poncho, sidelong smile, and strange homemade guitar.

—*Don McKay*

Bibliography

Hughes, Ted. *New Selected Poems, 1957–1994.* London: Faber and Faber, 1995.
Athanassakis, A.N., trans. *The Homeric Hymns.* Baltimore: Johns Hopkins University Press, 1976.

Acknowledgements

From *Air Occupies Space*
Windsor, ON: Sesame Press, 1973
    Down River, Into the Camp

From *Long Sault*
London, ON: Applegarth Follies, 1975
    At the Long Sault Parkway
    The Great Blue Heron

From *Lependu*
Ilderton, ON: Nairn Publishing, 1978
    The Eye Meets Tom Thomson's "A Rapid "
    The Trout
    August
    Lependu nearly materialized by his blackbirds

From *Birding, or Desire*
Toronto: McClelland and Stewart, 1983
    Field Marks:
    Leaving
    The Boy's Own Guide to Dream Birds
    I Scream You Scream
    Adagio for a Fallen Sparrow
    Field Marks (2):
    Identification

From *Sanding Down This Rocking Chair on a Windy Night*
Toronto: McClelland and Stewart, 1987
    Via, Eastbound
    Buckling
    Some Functions of a Leaf
    How to Imagine an Albatross

From *Night Field*
Toronto: McClelland and Stewart, 1991
    from Black Spruce
    Another Theory of Dusk
    Meditation on a Geode
    Choosing the Bow
    Meditation on Shovels
    Poplar

From *Apparatus*
Toronto: McClelland and Stewart, 1997
    Early Instruments
    Twinflower
    Alibi
    Materiel: (i) The Man from Nod
            (ii) Fates Worse Than Death
    Setting the Table: (i) Knife
               (ii) Fork
               (iii) Spoon
    Sometimes a Voice (1)
    Load
    Luna Moth Meditation
    Hush Factor
    Sometimes a Voice (2)

From *Varves*
Edmonton: Extra Virgin Chapbook Press, 2003
    Astonished

The Press would also like to acknowledge the help of Kitty Lewis and Adam Dickinson.

lps Books in the Laurier Poetry Series
Published by Wilfrid Laurier University Press